HOW TO ATTRACT MONEY
AND WEALTH
SPIRITUALLY

Spiritual steps to financial freedom

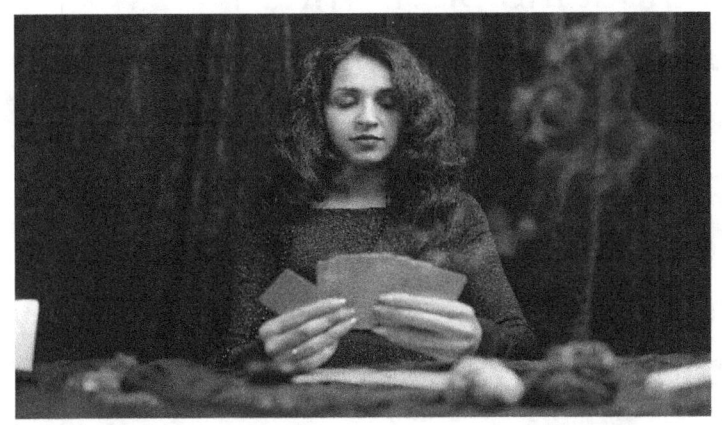

ABRAHAM WITE

TABLE OF CONTENTS

Introduction

Once, in a quaint town nestled between rolling hills, there lived a person named Alex who stumbled upon an old, dusty book in the hidden corner of the town's library. The cover bore the mysterious title, "The Alchemy of Abundance." Intrigued, Alex began reading the ancient wisdom within its pages.

As the words unfolded, a strange energy seemed to emanate from the book, enveloping Alex in an aura of positivity. Unbeknownst to them, the words held a secret power – a power to attract wealth and prosperity. The more Alex delved into the teachings, the more their life transformed.

Unexpected opportunities started knocking at Alex's door. Business ventures flourished, and unexpected windfalls graced their bank account. The once modest lifestyle evolved into one of opulence and abundance. People in the town marveled at Alex's newfound success, unaware of the enchanted book's influence.

However, as the riches poured in, so did the greed of those around Alex. Friends turned envious, and distant relatives sought a piece of the newfound wealth. The once-harmonious town now buzzed with jealousy and resentment.

Amidst this turmoil, Alex revisited the book, searching for a way to restore balance. The ancient text revealed a deeper truth — that true wealth lay not only in material abundance but also in sharing and uplifting others. Armed with this newfound wisdom, Alex embarked on a mission to use wealth for the betterment of the community.

Generosity replaced greed, and as Alex shared the knowledge from the magical book, the town underwent a transformation. Prosperity became a shared experience, and the once envious neighbors now worked together to create a thriving community.

In the end, Alex discovered that the true alchemy of abundance wasn't merely about attracting wealth but about using it wisely to foster a sense of prosperity for all. The enchanted book, though a catalyst, had imparted a lesson in the real magic of giving and community.

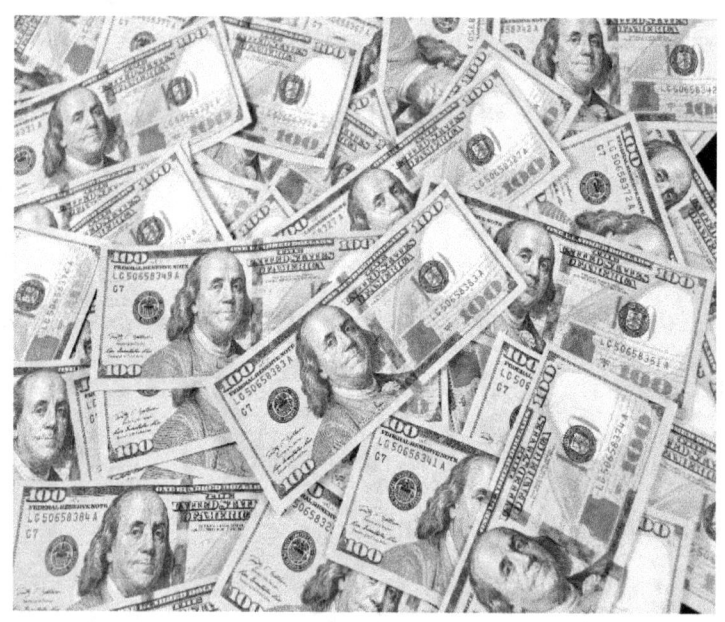

CHAPTER 1: Mindset and Beliefs

Mindset and Beliefs: Shaping Perspectives for Success

Mindset and beliefs are foundational elements that significantly influence how individuals perceive and navigate the world. These cognitive frameworks shape our thoughts, attitudes, and actions, playing a crucial role in personal development, decision-making, and overall well-being.

1. Understanding Mindset:

Fixed vs. Growth Mindset: Psychologist Carol Dweck introduced the concept of mindset, distinguishing between a fixed mindset and a growth mindset. A fixed mindset believes abilities are innate and unchangeable, while a growth mindset sees qualities as developable through effort and learning.

Impact on Learning: A growth mindset fosters resilience, a willingness to learn from failures, and a passion for improvement. Embracing challenges becomes a part of the learning journey, enhancing adaptability and perseverance.

2. Core Beliefs:

Formation and Influence: Beliefs are deeply rooted convictions about ourselves, others, and the world. These beliefs are often formed through personal experiences, cultural influences, and societal norms.

Limiting vs. Empowering Beliefs: Some beliefs can be limiting, creating self-imposed barriers and hindering personal growth. Empowering beliefs, on the other hand, propel individuals forward, instilling confidence and a sense of possibility.

3. The Interplay Between Mindset and Beliefs:

Reciprocal Relationship: Mindset and beliefs are interconnected; one influences the other. A growth mindset can lead to the adoption of empowering beliefs, while positive beliefs can reinforce a growth-oriented mindset.

Self-Fulfilling Prophecy: The beliefs individuals hold about their abilities can become self-fulfilling prophecies. Positive beliefs can boost confidence, leading to greater achievement, while negative beliefs may result in self-sabotage.

4. Cultivating a Positive Mindset and Empowering Beliefs:

Self-Awareness: Recognizing and understanding one's mindset and beliefs is the first step towards change. Reflecting on thought patterns and questioning limiting beliefs can pave the way for a more positive mindset.

Continuous Learning: Embracing a growth mindset involves a commitment to continuous learning. Viewing challenges as opportunities for growth and maintaining a curiosity-driven approach fosters a mindset geared towards improvement.

Affirmations and Visualization: Utilizing positive affirmations and visualization techniques can help reshape beliefs. By consistently reinforcing positive messages, individuals can reprogram their thought patterns and cultivate a more optimistic outlook.

5. Impact on Success and Well-Being:

Professional Success: A growth mindset and empowering beliefs are often correlated with professional success. Individuals who embrace challenges, persist in the face of setbacks, and believe in their ability to learn and adapt tend to excel in their careers.

Personal Fulfillment: Beyond professional achievements, mindset and beliefs contribute to personal fulfillment. A positive mindset can enhance overall well-being, relationships, and satisfaction with life.

In conclusion, mindset and beliefs are powerful influencers that shape the trajectory of our lives. By fostering a growth mindset and cultivating empowering beliefs, individuals can unlock their full potential, embrace challenges, and lead more fulfilling lives. The journey towards a positive mindset and empowering beliefs is a continuous process of self-discovery and intentional cultivation.

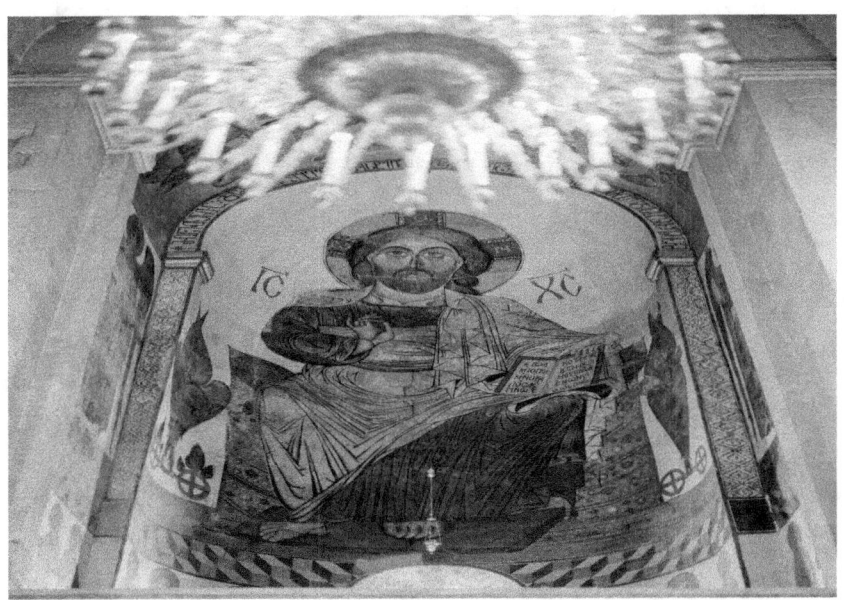

Understanding the Spiritual Connection to Wealth

Wealth, often associated with material abundance and financial prosperity, is a concept that extends beyond the tangible aspects of life. Many individuals find themselves on a quest for not only financial success but also a deeper, more meaningful connection to wealth through spiritual perspectives. Exploring this spiritual connection to wealth involves delving into various philosophical, religious, and metaphysical concepts that shed light on the interplay between spirituality and material prosperity.

Mindset and Manifestation:

At the core of the spiritual connection to wealth lies the concept of mindset and manifestation. Some spiritual traditions emphasize the power of thoughts and beliefs in shaping one's reality. The idea is that a positive and abundant mindset can attract wealth into one's life. This perspective aligns with the law of attraction, suggesting that focusing on positive thoughts can manifest positive outcomes, including financial success.

Karma and Ethical Wealth:

Many spiritual teachings, such as those found in Hinduism and Buddhism,

emphasize the importance of karma –
the law of cause and effect. From this
perspective, accumulating wealth
ethically and using it for the greater good
contributes to positive karma.
Understanding the spiritual connection to
wealth involves considering not just the
acquisition of wealth but also the ethical
implications of its pursuit and use.

Abundance Consciousness:

Abundance consciousness is a term
often used in spiritual circles to describe
an awareness of the infinite abundance
available in the universe. It suggests that
individuals can tap into this abundance
through a shift in consciousness, moving
away from a mindset of lack and scarcity.

Practices like meditation and gratitude are often recommended to cultivate abundance consciousness.

Sacred Economics:

Some spiritual perspectives view economics as a sacred aspect of life, intertwined with the broader cosmic order. This perspective encourages individuals to approach financial matters with a sense of reverence and responsibility, considering the impact of their financial decisions on both personal and collective well-being.

Material Detachment:

Spiritual teachings from various traditions often highlight the importance of detachment from material possessions. Understanding the spiritual connection to wealth involves finding a balance between material success and an awareness that true fulfillment transcends material acquisitions. This doesn't necessarily mean avoiding wealth but approaching it with a sense of detachment and understanding its impermanence.

Gratitude and Generosity:

Gratitude and generosity play vital roles in the spiritual connection to wealth. Expressing gratitude for current blessings, regardless of their scale, is seen as a way to attract more abundance. Additionally, acts of generosity are considered a means of circulating wealth and ensuring its flow, as opposed to hoarding it for personal gain.

Spiritual Practices for Prosperity:

Various spiritual practices are believed to enhance one's connection to wealth. Affirmations, visualization, and rituals specific to prosperity are common in spiritual traditions worldwide. These practices aim to align individuals with the energy of abundance and open them to receiving wealth in its various forms.

In conclusion, understanding the spiritual connection to wealth involves embracing a holistic perspective that goes beyond mere financial gain. It encompasses a mindset of abundance, ethical considerations, and a recognition of the interconnectedness of wealth with broader spiritual principles. By integrating these spiritual insights, individuals may find a deeper and more fulfilling relationship with wealth that goes beyond the material realm.

Importance of Aligning Spirituality and Money

Aligning spirituality and money is crucial for achieving a holistic and balanced life. While these two aspects may seem disparate, their integration can lead to enhanced well-being, purpose, and fulfillment. Here's a comprehensive exploration of the importance of aligning spirituality and money:

Values and Purpose:

- Integrating spirituality with financial decisions helps individuals identify and prioritize their core values. This alignment ensures that money is used in ways that resonate with one's deeper sense of purpose, fostering a more meaningful existence.

Mindful Spending:

- Spirituality encourages mindfulness, and this mindset can extend to financial habits. By aligning these two aspects, individuals become more conscious of their spending patterns, focusing on purchases that contribute to personal growth, well-being, and positive societal impact.

Reducing Materialism:

- Spirituality often emphasizes the transient nature of material possessions. Aligning with this perspective can lead to a reduced emphasis on accumulating material wealth for its own sake, fostering a healthier relationship with money that prioritizes experiences, relationships, and personal development.

Generosity and Giving:

- Many spiritual traditions emphasize the importance of generosity and giving back to the community. Aligning spirituality with financial decisions encourages individuals to allocate resources for charitable causes, contributing to the well-being of others and creating a sense of interconnectedness.

Financial Security and Peace of Mind:

- Integrating spirituality with money management can lead to a more balanced approach to financial security. Instead of excessive worry or attachment to wealth, individuals may find peace of mind in understanding that material possessions are not the ultimate source of fulfillment.

Career Alignment:

- Aligning spirituality and money can influence career choices. Individuals may seek professions that align with their values and contribute positively to society, even if it means sacrificing higher financial gains. This can lead to a more satisfying and purposeful professional life.

Stress Reduction:

- Financial stress is a common challenge, but spirituality provides tools for coping and resilience. By aligning these two aspects, individuals can develop a mindset that navigates financial challenges with greater equanimity, reducing stress and its adverse effects on mental and physical health.

Building Sustainable Wealth:

- Spiritual alignment encourages a focus on sustainable wealth-building practices. Instead of quick gains or exploitative financial strategies, individuals may adopt ethical and environmentally responsible approaches that consider the long-term impact of financial decisions.

Gratitude and Abundance Mindset:

- Many spiritual traditions emphasize gratitude and an abundance mindset. Aligning spirituality with money encourages individuals to appreciate what they have, fostering contentment and reducing the constant pursuit of more wealth as a source of happiness.

Personal Growth and Transformation:

- The alignment of spirituality and money can be a catalyst for personal growth and transformation. It invites individuals to explore their beliefs, challenge limiting financial beliefs, and embark on a journey of self-discovery that extends beyond material wealth.

In conclusion, the importance of aligning spirituality and money lies in creating a harmonious and purpose-driven life. This integration fosters a mindful and values-based approach to financial decisions, leading to personal fulfillment, societal contribution, and a balanced relationship with wealth.

Shifting Limiting Beliefs about Money

Introduction:

Limiting beliefs about money can significantly impact our financial well-being, hindering our ability to create wealth and achieve financial success. Shifting these beliefs is a crucial step toward cultivating a positive mindset and fostering a healthier relationship with money.

Understanding Limiting Beliefs:

Limiting beliefs are deeply ingrained convictions that shape our attitudes and behaviors toward money. These beliefs often stem from childhood experiences, societal influences, or past financial setbacks. Identifying and acknowledging these beliefs is the first step towards transformation.

Common Limiting Beliefs:

a. **Scarcity Mindset**: Believing that there's never enough money and that wealth is finite.

b. **Fear of Success**: Associating financial success with negative consequences or feeling undeserving of prosperity.

c. **Money is the Root of Evil**: Believing that pursuing wealth is morally wrong or leads to negative consequences.

Impact on Financial Behavior:

Limiting beliefs about money can manifest in various ways, such as overspending, avoiding financial opportunities, or staying in unfulfilling jobs due to fear of change. Understanding how these beliefs affect behavior is crucial for initiating change.

Challenging and Reframing Beliefs:

a. **Awareness**: Recognizing when limiting beliefs arise in thoughts or actions.

b. **Questioning**: Interrogating the validity of these beliefs and seeking evidence to the contrary.

c. **Affirmations**: Using positive affirmations to rewire the subconscious mind and replace negative beliefs with empowering ones.

Cultivating a Positive Money Mindset:

a. Gratitude Practice: Focusing on the positives in your financial life and expressing gratitude for what you have.

b. Visualization: Creating mental images of financial success and abundance to reprogram the mind.

c. Learning and Growth: Embracing financial education and viewing challenges as opportunities for personal and financial growth.

Seeking Professional Support:

Engaging with financial advisors, coaches, or therapists can provide valuable insights and guidance in challenging and overcoming limiting beliefs. These professionals can offer tailored strategies to address specific issues and provide ongoing support.

Creating Empowering Financial Habits:

Developing positive financial habits, such as budgeting, saving, and investing, reinforces a healthy money mindset. Consistent action towards financial goals helps build confidence and reinforces positive beliefs.

Measuring Progress:

Tracking and celebrating financial milestones, no matter how small, reinforces the positive changes and encourages continued growth. Regular reflection on progress helps solidify the shift in mindset.

Conclusion:

Shifting limiting beliefs about money is a transformative journey that requires self-awareness, commitment, and consistent effort. By challenging and reframing these beliefs, cultivating a positive money mindset, and seeking support when needed, individuals can break free from the constraints that hinder financial success and create a path toward lasting prosperity.

Cultivating an Abundance Mindset

Cultivating an abundance mindset is a transformative approach to life that involves shifting one's focus from scarcity to plenty. This mindset empowers individuals to see opportunities, appreciate successes, and embrace a positive outlook. Here's a comprehensive guide to cultivating an abundance mindset:

Understanding Abundance Mindset:

1. Definition: An abundance mindset is the belief that there are enough resources, opportunities, and successes to go around for everyone. It contrasts with a scarcity mindset, which fixates on limitations and fears a lack of resources.

2. Positive Outlook: Individuals with an abundance mindset view challenges as opportunities for growth. They see setbacks as temporary and believe in their ability to overcome obstacles.

Developing an Abundance Mindset:

1. Gratitude Practice:

   - Regularly express gratitude for what you have.

   - Reflect on positive aspects of your life to foster appreciation.

2. Positive Affirmations:

   - Use affirmations to reinforce positive beliefs about abundance.

- Replace negative self-talk with optimistic statements.

3. Embrace Challenges:

- See challenges as stepping stones to success.

- Focus on learning and growth during difficult times.

4. Learn from Failures:

- View failures as opportunities to learn and improve.

- Understand that setbacks are part of the journey to success.

5. Celebrate Others' Success:

- Cultivate joy for others' achievements.

- Recognize that someone else's success doesn't diminish your potential.

6. Visualization Techniques:

- Envision your goals and dreams becoming reality.

- Picture a future with abundance in various aspects of life.

Abundance in Relationships:

1. Generosity:

- Practice generosity and kindness towards others.

- Share knowledge, resources, and support with your community.

2. Build Connections:

- Network and build relationships with a diverse group of people.

- Embrace collaboration and mutual growth.

Abundance in Finances:

1. Financial Planning:

- Develop a strategic financial plan for long-term security.

- Focus on investment and wealth-building opportunities.

2. Money Mindset Shift:

- Replace a scarcity-driven fear of loss with a focus on financial growth.

- Believe in your ability to attract wealth and opportunities.

Abundance in Career:

1. Continuous Learning:

- Embrace a mindset of continuous improvement.

- Seek new skills and knowledge to stay competitive.

2. Opportunity Mindset:

- Approach challenges at work with a solution-oriented mindset.

- See setbacks as opportunities for career development.

Maintaining Abundance Mindset:

1. Mindfulness Practices:

- Engage in mindfulness meditation and self-reflection.

- Stay present and appreciate the abundance in the current moment.

2. Surround Yourself Positively:

- Choose to be around people who uplift and inspire.

- Limit exposure to negativity in media and social circles.

Cultivating an abundance mindset is an ongoing process that involves conscious effort and a commitment to positive thinking. By adopting these practices, individuals can reshape their perspectives, overcome limiting beliefs, and invite abundance into various aspects of their lives.

Chapter 2

Spiritual Practices for Manifestation: Cultivating Inner Power

In the journey of manifesting your desires, spiritual practices play a crucial role in aligning your energy with the universe. These practices not only help you connect with your inner self but also empower you to manifest your goals and dreams. Here's a comprehensive guide to spiritual practices for manifestation:

Meditation:

Meditation serves as the foundation for manifestation. Regular practice helps calm the mind, enhance focus, and raise your vibrational frequency, creating a conducive environment for manifesting your desires.

Visualization:

Envision your goals with vivid detail during meditation. Picture yourself living the life you desire. Visualization activates the law of attraction, attracting positive energies and opportunities.

Affirmations:

Craft positive, present-tense statements that reflect your desired reality. Repeating affirmations daily helps reprogram your subconscious mind, reinforcing beliefs that support your manifestations.

Gratitude Practice:

Expressing gratitude opens the door to abundance. Cultivate a habit of acknowledging and appreciating the positive aspects of your life. Gratitude amplifies the energy needed for manifestation.

Energy Clearing:

Release negative energies and emotions through practices such as smudging, energy healing, or simply spending time in nature. Clearing your energetic space creates room for manifestation energy to flow.

Law of Attraction Techniques:

Learn and apply the principles of the law of attraction. Understand that like attracts like and focus on positive thoughts and emotions to attract corresponding experiences into your life.

7. Crystal Healing:

Crystals carry unique energies that can enhance manifestation. Select crystals like citrine, amethyst, or clear quartz to amplify your intentions. Use them during meditation or carry them as talismans.

Moon Manifestation Rituals:

Harness the energy of the moon phases for manifestation. Set intentions during the new moon and release what no longer serves you during the full moon. The lunar cycle can be a powerful ally in your manifestation journey.

Journaling:

Maintain a manifestation journal to document your goals, progress, and gratitude. Reflecting on your journey helps reinforce your commitment and allows you to adjust your manifestations as needed.

Spiritual Connection:

Cultivate a deeper connection with your spiritual self, whether through prayer, rituals, or connecting with a higher power. This connection provides guidance and strength on your manifestation path.

Conclusion:

Embarking on a spiritual journey for manifestation requires consistency and an open heart. By integrating these practices into your daily life, you'll not only align with the energy of manifestation but also experience personal growth and a profound connection with the universe. Remember, the key lies in believing in your power to manifest and embracing the transformative journey within.

Visualization and affirmations

Visualization and affirmations are powerful tools that individuals often employ to enhance various aspects of their lives, including personal development, goal achievement, and overall well-being.

Visualization:

Visualization is a mental practice where individuals create vivid and detailed mental images of desired outcomes or goals. By engaging in this process, individuals aim to enhance their focus, motivation, and belief in their ability to achieve success. This technique is rooted in the idea that the mind and body are interconnected, and by consistently visualizing positive scenarios, individuals can positively influence their actions and outcomes.

Key Aspects of Visualization:

Clarity of Goals: Visualization works best when individuals have a clear understanding of their goals. By mentally picturing the desired outcomes, individuals can align their thoughts and actions with the path to success.

Emotional Engagement: Effective visualization involves not only seeing the end result but also feeling the associated emotions. Engaging the senses creates a more immersive mental experience, reinforcing the belief that the desired outcome is achievable.

Consistency: Regular practice is crucial for the effectiveness of visualization. Repeatedly visualizing goals strengthens neural pathways in the brain, making it more likely for individuals to subconsciously work towards those goals in their daily lives.lj

Affirmations:

Affirmations are positive statements that individuals repeat to themselves with the intention of cultivating a positive mindset, boosting self-esteem, and overcoming self-limiting beliefs. Affirmations can be written or spoken and are often personalized to address specific areas of improvement or personal development.

Key Aspects of Affirmations:

Positive Reinforcement: Affirmations serve as a form of positive self-talk. By consistently repeating positive statements, individuals reinforce a mindset that supports their goals and aspirations, counteracting negative thoughts or doubts.

Present Tense: Affirmations are most effective when phrased in the present tense, as if the desired outcome is already happening. This helps individuals shift their mindset from a distant goal to a current reality, fostering a sense of immediacy and belief in the attainability of their objectives.

Believability: It's essential for affirmations to be believable to the individual. Crafting statements that resonate with one's values and aspirations enhances the impact of affirmations, making them more likely to influence thoughts and behaviors.

Combining Visualization and Affirmations: The synergy between visualization and affirmations is potent. When used together, these practices create a comprehensive approach to personal development and goal attainment. Visualization sets the mental stage by creating a clear picture of success, while affirmations reinforce positive beliefs and attitudes necessary to manifest those visions into reality.

In conclusion, incorporating visualization and affirmations into daily routines can be a transformative practice. By leveraging the power of the mind through vivid imagery and positive affirmations, individuals can cultivate a mindset that aligns with their goals, ultimately paving the way for personal growth and success.

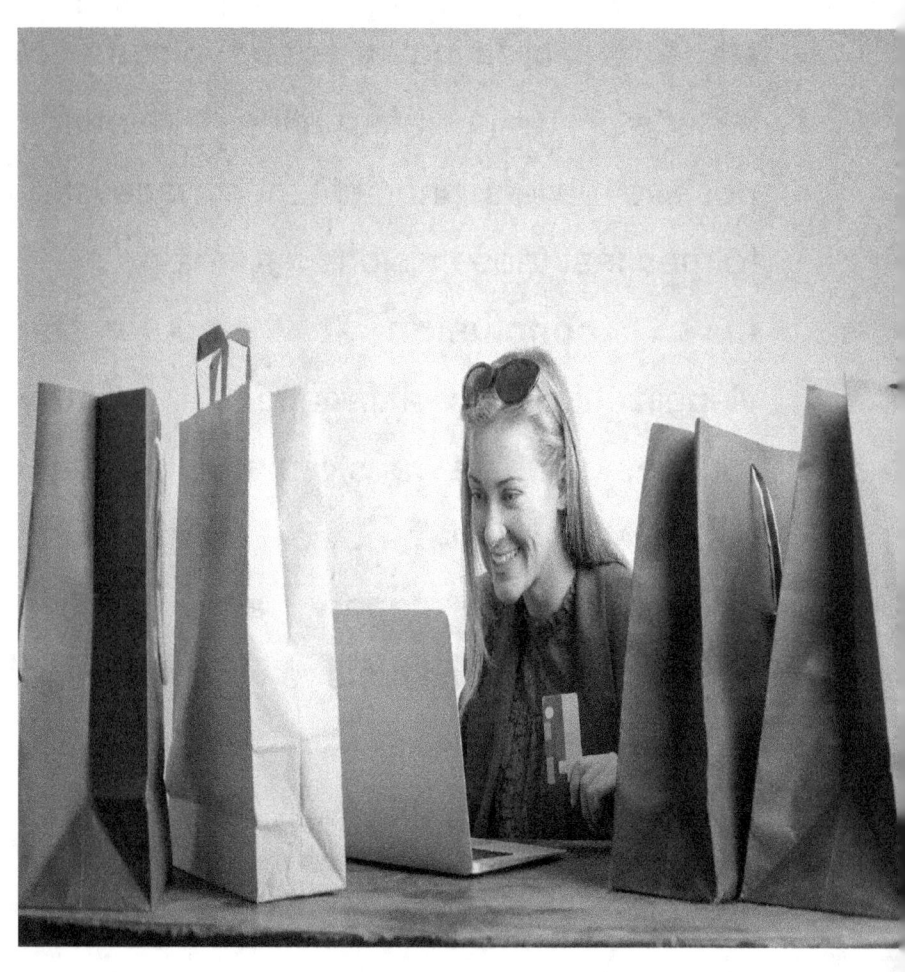

The Power of Meditation for Wealth Consciousness

Introduction:

In a world driven by material pursuits, the concept of wealth consciousness has gained prominence as individuals seek a holistic approach to abundance. One powerful tool that has emerged in this quest is meditation. Far beyond its traditional associations with spiritual practices, meditation has proven to be a transformative force in cultivating a mindset geared towards wealth and prosperity.

Understanding Wealth Consciousness:

Wealth consciousness goes beyond mere financial gain; it encompasses a mindset that attracts and appreciates abundance in all aspects of life. This mindset involves recognizing and releasing limiting beliefs about money, embracing abundance, and aligning oneself with the flow of prosperity.

The Role of Meditation:

1. Mindfulness Meditation:

-   Mindfulness meditation fosters awareness of thoughts and feelings related to wealth.

- By observing and understanding these thoughts without judgment, individuals can identify and reframe limiting beliefs.

2. Visualization Techniques:

- Visualization meditations involve mentally creating scenarios of wealth and success.

- This practice helps individuals become comfortable with the idea of abundance and trains the mind to attract positive outcomes.

3. Affirmations:

- Combining meditation with wealth-affirming statements can reshape thought patterns.

- Regular repetition of affirmations during meditation reinforces a positive and empowered wealth mindset.

Scientific Basis:

Meditation's impact on wealth consciousness is not purely metaphysical; scientific studies suggest tangible benefits. Meditation has been linked to reduced stress, improved decision-making, and increased focus—factors that contribute to a more conducive environment for wealth creation.

Developing a Meditation Routine:

1. Consistency:

- Regular meditation is key. Consistent practice helps embed the desired mindset over time.

2. Guided Meditations:

- Utilize guided meditations specifically designed for wealth consciousness to enhance the effectiveness of the practice.

3. Morning and Evening Rituals:

- Incorporating meditation into morning and evening routines sets a positive tone for the day and allows for reflection on achievements.

Real-life Success Stories:

Numerous individuals attribute their financial success to the integration of meditation into their daily lives. These stories serve as inspiration and testimony to the practical impact of meditation on wealth consciousness.

Conclusion:

Meditation for wealth consciousness is a holistic approach that transcends the conventional understanding of wealth. By combining mindfulness, visualization, and affirmations, individuals can reshape their relationship with money, paving the way for a mindset of abundance and prosperity. As meditation becomes an integral part of daily life, the journey towards unlocking wealth consciousness becomes a transformative and empowering experience.

Law of Attraction in Money Matters

The Law of Attraction, a metaphysical concept, posits that thoughts and feelings can attract corresponding experiences into one's life. When applied to money matters, this principle suggests that positive thoughts and emotions about wealth can attract financial success. Here's a comprehensive look at the Law of Attraction in relation to money:

Belief System:

   - Central to the Law of Attraction is the power of belief. Individuals are encouraged to cultivate a strong belief in their ability to attract financial abundance.

Positive Visualization:

- Visualization techniques involve vividly imagining financial success. This practice aims to align thoughts and emotions with the desired financial outcomes.

Affirmations:

- Affirmations are positive statements repeated regularly to reinforce a positive mindset about money. They are intended to reshape one's beliefs and attitudes toward wealth.

Gratitude Practice:

- Expressing gratitude for current financial circumstances, no matter how modest, is believed to attract more abundance. Gratitude is seen as a powerful magnet for positive energy.

Law of Reciprocity:

- The Law of Attraction often incorporates the law of reciprocity, emphasizing the idea that giving generously can lead to receiving abundantly. Acts of kindness and generosity are thought to create a positive flow of financial energy.

Emotional Alignment:

- Emotional alignment involves cultivating positive emotions related to money, such as joy, gratitude, and confidence. This alignment is considered crucial for attracting financial prosperity.

Detoxifying Negative Thoughts:

- Practitioners of the Law of Attraction strive to identify and eliminate negative thoughts and limiting beliefs about money. This process involves conscious efforts to replace negativity with positive affirmations.

Action as a Catalyst:

- While positive thinking is emphasized, the Law of Attraction doesn't discount the importance of taking action. Believers argue that positive thoughts should be accompanied by purposeful actions aligned with financial goals.

Quantum Physics Connection:

- Some proponents of the Law of Attraction draw connections to quantum physics, suggesting that thoughts and intentions can influence energy fields in ways that impact material reality, including financial outcomes.

Mindfulness Practices:

- Mindfulness techniques, such as meditation, are often recommended to enhance awareness and control over one's thoughts. These practices aim to foster a positive mental state conducive to attracting financial success.

Consistency and Patience:

- Applying the Law of Attraction to money matters requires consistency and patience. Believers argue that the manifestation of financial goals may take time, and maintaining a positive mindset throughout the journey is crucial.

Skepticism and Criticism:

- Despite its popularity, the Law of Attraction faces skepticism and criticism. Critics often highlight the lack of empirical evidence and caution against overlooking practical financial planning and hard work.

In conclusion, the Law of Attraction in money matters is a holistic approach that combines positive thinking, emotional alignment, and purposeful action to attract financial success. While it has fervent supporters, it's essential to approach it with an open mind, acknowledging the diversity of perspectives on its efficacy.

Chapter 3; Aligning Actions with Intentions

Aligning actions with intentions is a powerful concept that emphasizes the importance of ensuring one's behavior reflects their true goals and values. This process involves conscious decision-making and mindful awareness to bridge the gap between what one intends to achieve and how they actually behave.

Understanding Intentions:

1. Self-Reflection:

Begin by introspecting and understanding your core values and long-term goals. This self-awareness forms the foundation for aligning actions with intentions.

2. Clarity of Purpose:

Clearly define your intentions and objectives. Whether in personal relationships, career, or personal development, having a clear purpose provides a roadmap for your actions.

The Importance of Alignment:

1. Authenticity:

Aligning actions with intentions promotes authenticity. Being true to oneself fosters genuine connections with others and builds trust.

2. Reducing Cognitive Dissonance:

When actions deviate from intentions, it creates cognitive dissonance. Aligning them reduces internal conflict and enhances mental well-being.

Strategies for Alignment:

1. Mindfulness Practices:

Incorporate mindfulness techniques to stay present and conscious of your actions. This helps in making intentional choices rather than reacting impulsively.

2. Goal Setting:

Break down long-term intentions into actionable, measurable goals. This creates a roadmap, making it easier to align daily actions with overarching intentions.

3. Regular Check-Ins:

Periodically assess your actions in comparison to your intentions. Adjustments may be necessary as circumstances evolve.

Overcoming Challenges:

1. Identifying Obstacles:

Recognize potential barriers to alignment, such as external pressures or internal fears. Addressing these challenges is crucial for maintaining alignment.

2. Adaptability:

Life is dynamic, and circumstances change. Being adaptable allows you to realign actions with intentions when faced with unexpected challenges.

Benefits of Alignment:

1. Fulfillment:

Living in accordance with your intentions fosters a sense of fulfillment and purpose. It creates a meaningful and satisfying life.

2. Improved Relationships:

Alignment enhances communication and understanding in relationships. Consistency between intentions and actions builds stronger connections.

Real-Life Examples:

1. Professional Development:

Aligning actions with career goals involves making strategic decisions, continuous learning, and networking to progress in the desired direction.

2. Healthy Lifestyle:

Intentions for a healthy lifestyle can be realized through daily habits like exercise, balanced nutrition, and sufficient sleep.

Conclusion:

Aligning actions with intentions is a lifelong process that requires self-awareness, commitment, and adaptability. It is a transformative journey that not only enhances individual well-being but also positively influences the world by fostering authenticity and genuine connections.

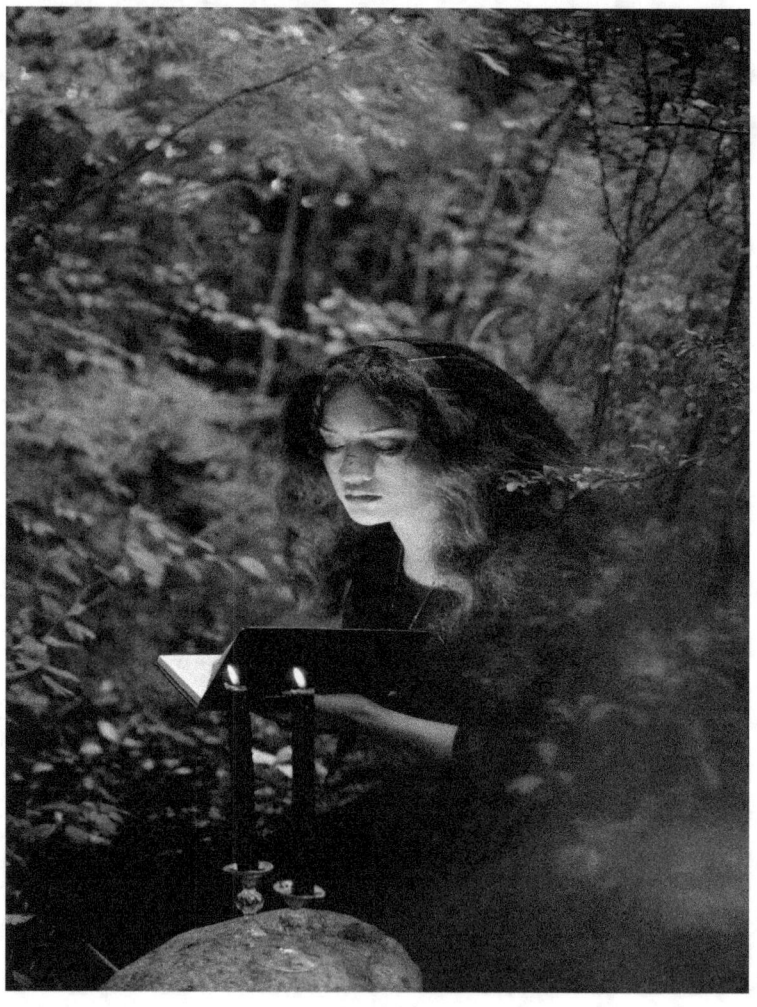

Setting Financial Goals with Purpose

Setting financial goals with purpose is a crucial aspect of personal financial management. Purposeful goals provide direction, motivation, and a clear roadmap for achieving financial success. Here's a comprehensive guide to help you establish and pursue financial goals with intention:

Reflect on Your Values:

Start by identifying your core values and what truly matters to you. This reflection will guide you in setting goals that align with your priorities, ensuring a sense of fulfillment as you work towards them.

Define Short-Term and Long-Term Objectives:

Categorize your financial goals into short-term and long-term objectives. Short-term goals could include building an emergency fund or paying off credit card debt, while long-term goals may involve saving for retirement or purchasing a home.

Be Specific and Measurable:

Clearly define each goal with specific details and measurable criteria. For example, instead of a vague goal like "save money," specify an amount and a timeframe, such as "save $5,000 in the next 12 months."

Prioritize Goals:

Rank your financial goals in order of importance. This helps you focus on what matters most, especially when faced with limited resources or unexpected challenges.

Create an Action Plan:

Break down each goal into smaller, manageable steps. Develop a realistic action plan that outlines the tasks you need to accomplish to reach your objectives. This enhances accountability and makes the journey less overwhelming.

Consider SMART Criteria:

Ensure your goals are Specific, Measurable, Achievable, Relevant, and Time-Bound. This framework provides a structured approach, increasing the likelihood of successful goal attainment.

Review and Adjust:

Regularly review your financial goals and track your progress. Be open to adjusting them based on changes in your life, financial situation, or priorities. Flexibility is key to staying on course.

Involve Family and Seek Professional Advice:

If applicable, involve family members in the goal-setting process. Their support and input can be valuable. Additionally, consider seeking advice from financial professionals to ensure your goals are realistic and aligned with your overall financial plan.

Celebrate Milestones:

Acknowledge and celebrate your achievements along the way. Recognizing milestones boosts motivation and reinforces positive financial habits.

Stay Committed and Persistent:

Financial goals require commitment and persistence. Stay focused on your objectives, even when faced with challenges. The journey may have ups and downs, but a purposeful mindset will help you navigate through them.

In **conclusion**, setting financial goals with purpose involves aligning your aspirations with your values, creating a well-defined plan, and staying adaptable throughout the journey. By integrating purpose into your financial goals, you not only enhance your financial well-being but also contribute to a more meaningful and fulfilling life.

Taking Inspired Action: Unleashing Potential and Achieving Goals

Taking inspired action involves more than mere motivation; it's a dynamic process fueled by passion, purpose, and a profound connection to one's goals. This comprehensive guide explores the essence of taking inspired action, the steps involved, and the transformative impact it can have on personal and professional growth.

Understanding Inspired Action

Inspired action stems from a deep sense of purpose and inner motivation. It goes beyond the routine and taps into a wellspring of creativity and enthusiasm. Unlike forced actions, inspired actions are aligned with one's values and vision, propelling individuals towards meaningful achievements.

Key Elements of Inspired Action

1. Clarity of Purpose:

-    Define your goals clearly, understanding the why behind each objective.

- Align your actions with your values and long-term vision.

2. Mindful Awareness:

- Cultivate mindfulness to stay present and fully engaged in the current task.

- Recognize opportunities and remain open to new possibilities.

3. Passion and Motivation:

- Identify activities that genuinely ignite your passion.

- Connect with your intrinsic motivation to sustain momentum.

4. Overcoming Fear and Resistance:

- Acknowledge and confront fears that may hinder progress.

- Embrace discomfort as a sign of growth and push through resistance.

5. Strategic Planning:

- Develop a realistic action plan with achievable milestones.

- Break down larger goals into smaller, manageable tasks.

The Process of Taking Inspired Action

1. Visualization:

- Create a vivid mental image of your desired outcomes.

- Visualizing success enhances belief and commitment.

2. Set Intentions:

- Clarify your intentions before taking any action.

- Ensure your actions align with your overarching goals.

3. Continuous Learning:

- Stay curious and seek knowledge related to your pursuits.

- Learning fuels inspiration and provides valuable insights.

4. Adaptability:

- Embrace flexibility and be willing to adjust your approach.

- Adaptation allows for resilience in the face of challenges.

5. Celebrate Progress:

- Acknowledge and celebrate small victories along the way.

- Positive reinforcement enhances motivation and commitment.

Benefits of Taking Inspired Action

1. Fulfillment:

- Engaging in activities aligned with your passions brings a deep sense of fulfillment.

2. Innovation and Creativity:

- Inspired actions often lead to innovative solutions and creative breakthroughs.

3. Increased Resilience:

- The intrinsic motivation behind inspired action fosters resilience in the face of setbacks.

4. Heightened Productivity:

- A clear sense of purpose and motivation enhances focus and productivity.

Conclusion

Taking inspired action is a transformative journey that requires self-awareness, passion, and strategic planning. By aligning actions with a clear sense of purpose and staying committed to personal growth, individuals can unlock their true potential and achieve meaningful success in various aspects of life. It's not just about doing more; it's about doing what truly matters, driven by inspiration and purpose.

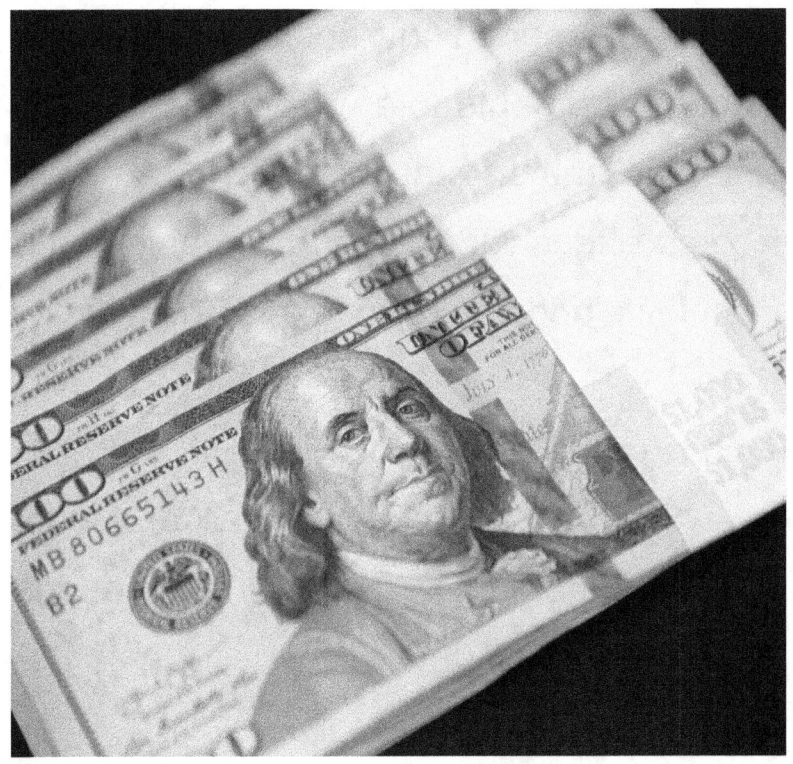

Creating a Positive Money Flow

Creating a positive money flow is crucial for financial stability and growth. It involves managing income, expenses, and investments in a way that ensures a surplus rather than a deficit. Here's a comprehensive guide to help you achieve and maintain a positive money flow:

Budgeting:

- Start by creating a detailed budget that outlines your monthly income and expenses.

- Categorize expenses into fixed (e.g., rent, utilities) and variable (e.g., groceries, entertainment).

- Allocate a portion of your income for savings and emergency funds.

Emergency Fund:

- Establish an emergency fund to cover unexpected expenses, such as medical bills or car repairs.

- Aim for 3-6 months' worth of living expenses in your emergency fund to provide a financial safety net.

- Prioritize paying off high-interest debts to reduce financial burden.

- Explore debt consolidation options or negotiate with creditors for better terms.

Increase Income:

- Look for opportunities to enhance your income, such as taking on a side hustle or investing in skill development.

- Consider negotiating a raise at your current job or exploring new career opportunities.

Expense Reduction:

- Identify areas where you can cut expenses without sacrificing essential needs.

- Negotiate bills, shop smartly, and avoid unnecessary subscriptions.

Investing:

- Diversify your investments to build wealth over time.

- Consider a mix of stocks, bonds, and real estate based on your risk tolerance and financial goals.

Savings Automation:

- Set up automatic transfers to your savings and investment accounts to ensure consistent contributions.

- Take advantage of employer-sponsored retirement plans and other investment vehicles.

Financial Education:

- Stay informed about personal finance and investment strategies.

- Continuously educate yourself on ways to optimize your financial decisions.

Insurance Coverage:

- Ensure you have adequate insurance coverage for health, property, and life to protect against unforeseen circumstances.

- Regularly review and update your insurance policies as needed.

Long-Term Planning:

- Develop a long-term financial plan, including retirement goals and major expenses.

- Adjust your plan periodically to adapt to changes in income, expenses, and life circumstances.

Mindful Spending:

- Practice mindful spending by distinguishing between needs and wants.

- Avoid impulsive purchases and make informed decisions about your expenditures.

Regular Financial Checkups:

- Schedule regular reviews of your financial situation to track progress and make adjustments.

- Seek professional advice if needed, especially for complex financial matters.

By incorporating these strategies into your financial routine, you can create a positive money flow that not only meets your current needs but also secures a stable and prosperous future.

Chapter 4 Gratitude and Abundance

Gratitude and abundance are interconnected concepts that emphasize a positive and appreciative mindset towards life. Gratitude involves acknowledging and expressing thankfulness for the positive aspects of one's life, fostering a sense of contentment and satisfaction. It is a powerful tool for cultivating a positive outlook, enhancing mental well-being, and building stronger relationships.

Abundance, on the other hand, goes beyond material wealth. It encompasses a mindset of plenty, recognizing the richness of life in various forms, such as love, opportunities, experiences, and personal growth. Adopting an abundance mindset involves believing in the inherent possibilities and opportunities that surround us, leading to a more fulfilling and purposeful life.

Practicing gratitude involves taking time to reflect on and appreciate the good things in life, both big and small. It can be as simple as keeping a gratitude journal, where individuals jot down things they are thankful for each day. This practice has been linked to improved mental health, reduced stress, and increased overall life satisfaction.

An abundance mindset involves shifting focus from scarcity to plenty. Instead of dwelling on what is lacking, individuals with an abundance mindset recognize and appreciate the abundance that already exists in their lives. This mindset encourages creativity, risk-taking, and a positive approach to challenges, fostering resilience in the face of setbacks.

The relationship between gratitude and abundance is symbiotic. When individuals cultivate gratitude, they often attract more positive experiences and opportunities, contributing to a sense of abundance. Conversely, adopting an abundance mindset can enhance one's ability to be grateful, as the focus shifts from what is lacking to the abundance that is present.

In daily life, incorporating gratitude and abundance can involve mindfulness practices, such as meditation or reflection, to consciously appreciate the present moment. Acts of kindness and generosity towards others also contribute to a sense of abundance by creating positive connections and fostering a spirit of giving.

In summary, gratitude and abundance are integral components of a positive and fulfilling life. By cultivating gratitude, individuals can experience increased well-being and satisfaction. Adopting an abundance mindset further amplifies these benefits, creating a mindset that attracts and recognizes the abundance that exists in various aspects of life. Together, these practices can lead to a more positive and enriching life journey.

Practicing Gratitude for Current Finances

Practicing gratitude for your current finances can have a positive impact on both your mental well-being and financial habits. By cultivating a grateful mindset, you can foster contentment, reduce stress, and make more informed financial decisions.

Introduction:
Gratitude is a powerful emotion that extends beyond personal relationships to encompass various aspects of life,

including finances. Acknowledging and appreciating your current financial situation can lead to a more positive outlook and improved financial behaviors.

Understanding Gratitude in Finances: Gratitude in finances involves recognizing the positive aspects of your current financial state, whether it's having a stable income, meeting basic needs, or achieving financial goals. It's about shifting focus from what you lack to what you have.

Benefits of Practicing Gratitude for Finances:

Reduced Stress: Gratitude helps alleviate financial stress by emphasizing what is going well rather than dwelling on challenges.

- **Improved Mental Well-being:** Cultivating gratitude has been linked to enhanced mental health, contributing to better decision-making and emotional resilience.

Enhanced Financial Mindfulness: Grateful individuals are often more mindful of their spending and saving habits, leading to more responsible financial choices.

Practical Strategies for Cultivating Gratitude:

- **Gratitude Journaling:** Regularly jot down aspects of your financial life that you are thankful for, such as a steady job, supportive networks, or meeting budgetary goals.

Reflection on Progress: Take time to reflect on financial milestones achieved, whether it's paying off debt, saving for a specific goal, or building an emergency fund.

Mindful Spending and Saving:

Conscious Consumption: Practice gratitude by being mindful of your purchases and appreciating the value they bring to your life.

- **Saving with Purpose:** Save with a sense of gratitude for future financial security, acknowledging the positive impact of disciplined saving habits.

Building Resilience in Financial Challenges:

- **Gratitude in Adversity:** During tough financial times, focus on what resources and support you have rather than fixating on difficulties, fostering resilience.

Cultivating a Gratitude Mindset as a Long-Term Strategy:

Consistent Practice: Integrate gratitude into your daily routine to make it a sustainable and impactful habit.

- **Sharing Gratitude:** Express appreciation for financial support or advice from others, reinforcing a positive financial community.

Conclusion:

Practicing gratitude for your current finances is not about ignoring challenges but rather approaching them with a positive and appreciative mindset. It can lead to a healthier relationship with money, improved financial decision-making, and a greater sense of overall well-being. Embracing gratitude in your financial journey is a valuable and transformative practice.

Attracting Abundance through Appreciation

Attracting abundance through appreciation involves cultivating a mindset of gratitude and recognizing the positive aspects of one's life. By acknowledging and valuing the present moment, individuals can create a magnetic energy that attracts prosperity and abundance. Here's a comprehensive look at the key principles and practices associated with this concept:

1. Gratitude as a Foundation:

-**Recognition of Blessings**: Start by acknowledging and appreciating the existing blessings in your life, both big and small.

- **Shift in Perspective**: Cultivate a mindset that focuses on what you have rather than what you lack.

2. Law of Attraction:

- **Positive Energy Magnetism**: The law of attraction suggests that positive thoughts and feelings attract positive experiences. Appreciation generates positive energy, aligning your vibration with abundance.

3. Mindfulness Practices:

- **Present Moment Awareness**: Engage in mindfulness techniques to stay present, allowing appreciation for the current circumstances.

- **Daily Gratitude Journaling**: Regularly document things you are grateful for to reinforce a positive mindset.

4. Affirmations and Visualization:

- **Positive Affirmations**: Use affirmations that reflect gratitude and abundance to program your subconscious mind.

- **Visualization Techniques**: Imagine and feel the abundance you desire as if it is already present in your life.

5. Generosity and Giving:

- **Law of Reciprocity**: Give freely without expecting anything in return. The act of giving creates a flow of positive energy.

- **Abundance Mindset**: Generosity reinforces the belief in abundance, breaking the scarcity mindset.

6. Appreciation in Relationships:

- Expressing Gratitude: Communicate your appreciation to others, strengthening personal and professional relationships.

- **Positive Connection**: Building positive connections enhances the flow of abundance in various aspects of life.

7. Self-Love and Self-Appreciation:

- **Valuing Personal Worth**: Recognize and appreciate your unique qualities and talents.

- **Positive Self-Talk**: Replace self-criticism with self-affirmation to foster a sense of worthiness.

8. Abundance Rituals:

-**Gratitude Rituals**: Create daily or weekly rituals that center around expressing gratitude.

-**Manifestation Practices**: Combine gratitude with specific manifestation practices to amplify the attraction of abundance.

9. Continuous Learning and Growth:

- **Adopting a Growth Mindset**: Embrace challenges as opportunities for growth, appreciating the journey.

- **Learning from Setbacks**: View setbacks as lessons, maintaining a positive outlook even in challenging times.

10. Consistency and Patience:

- **Persistent Practice**: Attracting abundance through appreciation is a continuous practice.

- **Patience and Trust**: Trust the process and be patient, allowing the universe to unfold in its own time.

In summary, attracting abundance through appreciation involves a holistic approach that encompasses gratitude, positive energy, mindfulness, generosity, and self-love. By integrating these principles into daily life, individuals can create a powerful mindset that magnetizes abundance in various forms.

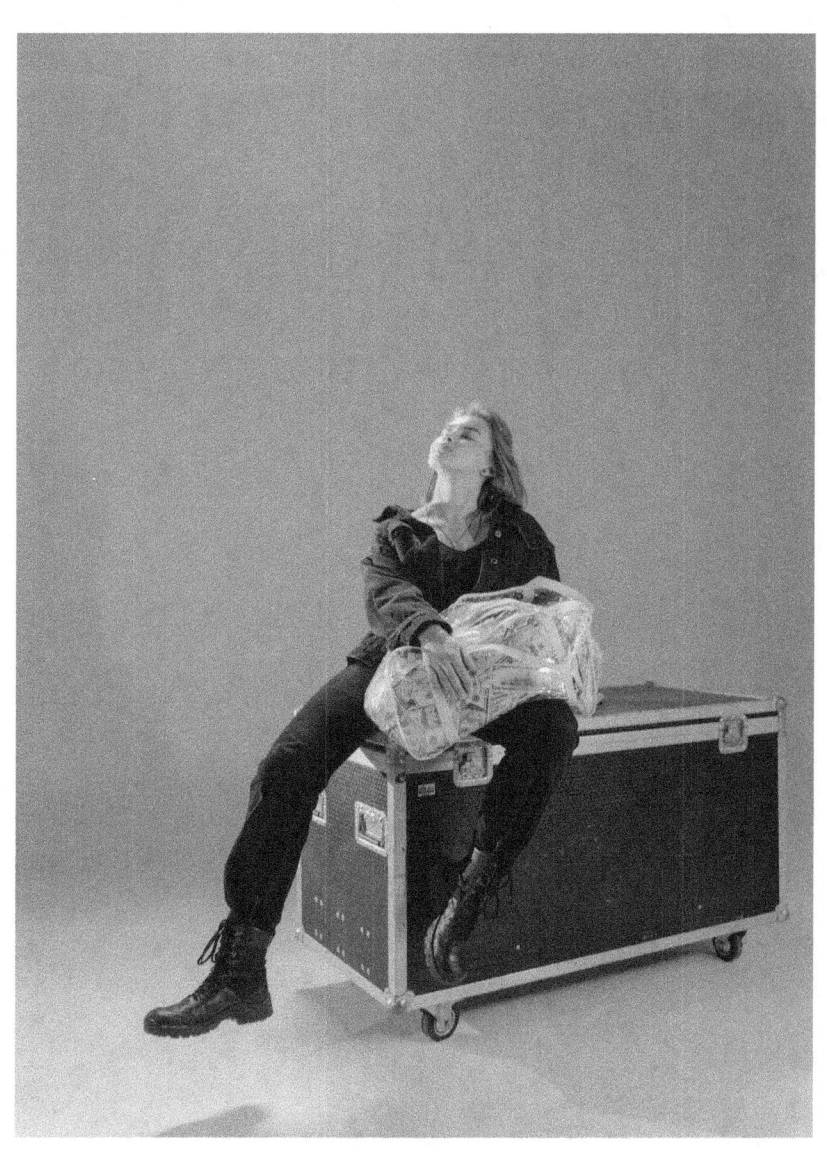

www.ingramcontent.com/pod-product-compliance
Lightning Source LLC
Chambersburg PA
CBHW062331290526
45794CB00005B/1996